To Tasha,

A guide to the future

Best wishes

Don

A Clear Imagination

~ Don Garrett ~

Published by

MELROSE BOOKS

An Imprint of Melrose Press Limited
St Thomas Place, Ely
Cambridgeshire
CB7 4GG, UK
www.melrosebooks.com

FIRST EDITION

Copyright © Don Garrett 2008

The Author asserts his moral right to
be identified as the author of this work

Cover designed by Catherine McIntyre

ISBN 978-1-906050-62-7

Printed and bound in Great Britain by:
Biddles. King's Lynn. Norfolk PE30 4LS

Mixed Sources

Product group from well-managed
forests, controlled sources and
recycled wood or fiber
www.fsc.org Cert no. TT-COC-002303
© 1996 Forest Stewardship Council

PEFC
PEFC/16-33-293
PEFC · Promoting Sustainable Forest Management

Should you recognize yourself in these poems or indeed find them somewhat amusing, then I thank you for your generosity in purchasing "A Clear Imagination."

Some of my works may cause emotions to reignite, I do not apologize for this because I wrote as I felt at that moment in time.

I too had tears in my eyes, the hairs rising on the back of my neck and goose pimples; hopefully you will too for if you do then you are indeed an emotional, wonderful and lovable person.

In dedicating this book to my daughters Samantha and Rebecca I have allowed my emotions to run free in the hope that I have captured the essence of the love and closeness we had between us.

It is because of them that I was shown how to tell through words, the pain and heartache of a break down of a marriage, I know not the effect it has on my daughters I can only hope that this book will somehow ease their troubled minds and allow them to realise that their Dad will always love and be there for them.

A Clear Imagination

As the girth steadily grows wider
And the once strong legs begin to bow
The firm straight back slowly bends over
While the hands fumble and loose their grip

Whilst the mind plays up and begins to flit
Looking through the young eyes in an old head
Just knowing what we want to say
Yet something else comes out instead

The stairs seem much steeper now
As you climb them to go to bed
It looks quite light outside you think
Forgetting that it is daytime instead

The whole thing seems so exhausting as you try to catch your breath
You weren't like this yesterday for the mind is very clear
Sharp as the razor blade you used all through last year
Cataracts impede the vision, no on your glasses there is a smear

The silence is broken only, by the soft ticking of the clock
A cloud of dust arises as you shuffle across the floor
The once firm tread has gone now just the slippers and the sock
The hearing is slowly going, was that a knock upon the door?

No I'm not getting older this said with a firm and steady grip
Passing time just clouds the issue plants thoughts inside the head
Why it seems like only yesterday I was sailing on my ship
I'm very sure of everything for that is what the nurse just said

A Cloak of Sadness

So rare is the beauty that I have found in you
Although a cloak of sadness, I think that you look through
What secrets deep inside you hold, is joy for you forbidden?
Is happiness denied to you entrapped behind a manikin of alabaster hue?

Desires, emotions and deep feelings refrained from ever being true?
If once in time, enjoyment calls and offers you a smile of understanding
The door of happiness opens calls and beckons you to enter through
Always your footsteps falter at the door, to the secret, you must be true

Will you forever stay in darkness, with a heart heavy, full of pain?
A spirit young, so full of vigour, looks for love to be the trigger
Strong ties from time now long since gone, calls to you their creation
Chains of burden do weigh you down full of fear and pain you do not flicker

The empty, lonely walk through life has placed you on the path of isolation
Yet through the dark and sadness glows, a flame which could burn fierce and bright
Recognised and welcomed by only you through hunger, yearning and delight
So in the shadows you should no longer dwell, the heartache now you could dispel

Your eyes showed me a heart so pure; go now enjoy the love which breaks the spell
In searching for a friendly soul, one who will share your darkened path
Where strength of mind and stout of heart, hands held fast no fear will show
Head held high, belief burns bright, embodiment of a love forever to last
Through turmoil wracked by ravaged ghosts, clear pure thoughts cannot flow

A Cloud is her Whisper

It has come now the time has expired
Whatever you wanted has now disappeared,
How deep is the shadow, how large is the soul?
To carry forever a burden so cold.

No courage is needed as strength will prevail.
A cloud is her whisper the wind is her kiss,
The sun is her being that caresses your skin,
The moon is her temple ghostly white does it shine

The stars are her eyes brightly glowing divine,
The rain is her teardrops she sheds with no sin.
Haunting memories become crystal clear
Needing no prompting, they want to be here,

Forgoing the future recalling only the past
Treading cold footsteps not following a path
In front there's a signpost walk on with no fear.
A chill is on the wind, a frost upon the breath

An echo of a footfall upon an empty street.
The senses begin to tingle awake to every creak
Eyes staring in the distance her in vision you must keep.
Closer now in distance her perfume pervades the air

In silent anticipation the longing to hold her if you dare
Two echoes now of footfalls, two shadows merge as one
A warm smile of recognition your love for that she has won.

A Comforting Hug

It is a very personal thing for just you two
Arms that embrace and holds gently onto you
Warm and so tender an arc of delightful protection
It is what you needed, keeps you from isolation.

A man needs a comforting hug every now and again
Stops them being macho, just keeps them quite simply, sane.
It means such a lot to know that you are loved and needed
A gesture so simple so pure, over indulgence is never exceeded.

The warmth of your woman the smell of her hair
When leaving her embrace it is very hard to bear,
The look of love from her eyes brings a flush to her cheek
While inside of you the feelings have yet to reach their peak.

So life for you can be good and sometimes it can be cruel,
Depending on your standing as nobodies fool.
Should you be as sharp as the pin or smooth as the silk?
The whole of life's pleasures you should enjoyingly milk.

Yes a hug is a wonderful, comforting warming thing
Spontaneity without thought, has the essential ring
Showing emotions actually comes from deep in the heart
Being bold and being brash gives romance that extra part.

A Delicate Balance

When the world passes by the window
All clad in their silk and colourful refinery
Whilst sitting at the table calculating out the binary
The hollow silence echoes just to let you know.

Each person has a choice of path along which to tread
Surrounded by the four walls not speaking to a soul
Sliding down the spiral how swiftly you have sped
Looking at the bad deeds done and to those you can't console,

Past life flashes by showing the style of life you once led
Trials and tribulations and the wrongs you wish to right.
Gorging yourself from the festive plate, ignoring those you could have fed
Does time allow for errors or have we become life's parasite?

Looking out of sightless eyes and turning a deaf ear
Walking away from the poor, those who are most needy
Grasping eagerly at every cent this makes you very greedy
Yet deep inside something stirs, unknown and quite unclear

So deeply troubled but not yet in a stressful mode
Seeking out the stranger destiny arranged for you to meet
A hushed conversation that guides you to the right road
Soft whispers give you the secret forever you must keep.

A Delightful Slumber

Slumber awhile longer for now we are together side by side,
The comfort you have given will be forever repaid in kind
Upon receiving your friendship life has turned around with a smile
A welcoming morning follows the comfort of night now eases the mind.

While resting your head upon a pillow are your thoughts set free
Does your heart swell with yearning for that which used to be?
When love was the cornerstone and happiness seemed so very dear
Now lying with your mind awake these feelings are more sincere and clear.

Stay a little longer or at least until the sun again does shine
Let us try to understand what love is and follow all the signs
When night descends upon us and close together we become
For as natural as the world spins so we become as one.

And from your dreams a fleeting look into the future
Yet in the idyllic sleepiness just as dreams are there by chance
An envelope of warmth and comfort to stretch enjoy and enhance
The delightful slumber with your chosen one of whom you are so sure.

A Dream

Don't tread upon my dreams that way
Let me sleep a little longer for it is in the twilight time that my visions
Become that much clearer
Here I can hold and see all that is dear to me

Where I find love and comfort
Here I can see that which I helped to create.
I see how by giving all my love
I made sure that you could survive

For I am no longer there to guide and protect you
No longer can I learn from you, or able to teach you.
A memory lies within my mind
Pictures of you when I knew you

But we both have changed
You matured, me getting older.
The eyes see differently now no longer admiration
But scorn and disassociation doubt and vilification

Love is an eternity away
No longer a smile of welcome to stay.
A shattered mirror shows images altered
No clear reflection of the truth just a broken dream

A scratch from a shard draws blood, which can be stemmed
Inside a broken heart is hidden, no blood just pain.
Upon your birth my life changed forever
I saw a miracle that took my breath away

So fragile yet so strong, so tiny yet so loud
My future vision of a family so clear and crisp in the morning light
Joy and amazement wonder and disbelief, emotions all mixed up.
I see you at night asleep secure with the knowledge that I am there

How many nights did I look at you my creation, what dreams I had
How I loved you, to infinity and beyond.

A Dusty Identity

Upon the top shelf now long forgotten just collecting dust
A funny old object appears to be covered in rust
Although it is not made of metal or plastic nor zinc;
It's there covered in cobwebs about half an inch deep.

Surrounded by boxes and various odds and ends
Untouched for ages and the shape never blends,
Sitting in darkness and out of harms way
Once held as a treasure on someone's birthday;

Like all materialistic objects the sheen always in time dims
For a momentary pleasure is accepted as one of those things.
So it is stored in a safe place where we know where it is
Ready for a surprise showing when the time comes for glitz.

Now here we are and the years did swiftly fly
Upon moving house whilst packing it's found by and by.
This funny shaped object now sparkling all free of dust
Has pride of place in the new home a familiar known bust.

A Fair Prospect

I cannot tell the sweetness of your kiss for I have not tasted your lips,
I cannot tell of the warmth of your hands for I have not touched your skin.
I cannot tell of the feelings within your heart for I have not got close to you,
I cannot tell of how you think of me for I have not looked deep into your eyes.

A time will come when I will tell all for as the sun rises so shall our love,
To blossom as the spring flowers, to be as joyful as the new born lambs,
Excited at the prospect of going forward now with you by my side
Where the horizon is infinity so shall my love be, for within I feel as one.

The inner peace I have is like a bolt of silk, smooth, cool and nice to feel.
No wrinkles to cheat the skin, the suppleness and sheen caress the flesh,
Though you may never read my words for the time is still to come before it's real
So I write what I think is right and with hope and love in my heart for you to possess.

A Far Away Place

Did the look mean so much?
Did the smile though warm and inviting
Stir forgotten emotions once again?
Did the eyes linger a little bit longer?

Make the pulse beat that little bit stronger?
A fleeting look as she passes by, a ghost of a smile
Captured for eternity in the mind's eye,
Her perfume wafts around your head for a while

Intoxicates, exhilarates makes you alive.
A dream in a far away place
Stimulates accelerates soothes and calms
Banishes weariness, adds a belief

Encourages, instils a silence within
Fuels a hunger deep down eager to taste.
Emptiness surrounds you an image in mist
The ache in the head, the mouth has no taste

Longing for the moment one cannot resist
As a hand reaches out, gently touches the face.
Imprinted forever in weather-beaten skin
Holding together an imaginary thing

The silence forever no cardinal sin
A dream with no spirit, no earthly thing.
To capture a moment and hold it so dear
Tenderly caressing the beauty that is so near

In raptures of pleasure so pleasing to see
Awaiting the kiss to set your heart free.

A Glance

The passing look of tenderness
The liquid pool of tears,
The trail of the teardrop
Gently rolling down the cheek

The tightness of the throat
Makes us incapable of speech.
The head thrown back
Hair over the shoulder

Out the corner of ones eye
She asks you to be bolder.
Is this as plain as can be
Is this directed just at me?

I'm getting hot around the collar
It's so tight I cannot swallow.
I'll pluck up the courage
And take a big chance

I'll approach her quite swiftly
And ask her to dance.
Out on the dance floor
Our bodies do gel

Each contour adjoining
As they only knew well.
The mood of the music
Is sensuous enough

The togetherness of our bodies
Feels like the electrical stuff.
Could this be the natural spark?
To start love flowing, soaring like the lark,

The music is still playing
And the bodies are still swaying.
The tempo and the beat are moving our feet
While our eyes dine with delight

Hands gently clasped, breath comes in gasps
Is this reality finally, at last?
Knowing that love can arrive with just a glance.

A Late Proposal

Have I missed you? Am I too late?
There isn't enough time left to appreciate
Days spent together and sharing the load.
Watching the sunsets together as we grow old.

Meeting so late missing our youth
Not mellowing together, not learning the truth
Nights are so lonely barren and bare
Nobody there to show that they care.

If I had a wish that I'd like to come true
It would be that I could spend more time with you
On a day that is special your whole life through
Is the day that we become husband and wife.

A Memory of Senses

It was the look in the eye as the light danced to the smile
A flick of the hair to make her beguile
The nape of the neck, a brief sensuous glimpse
As she passed by, a sway of the hips.

The fragrance of her perfume lingered as it closed around my head
Words were not spoken, nothing was ever said
Eyes watched as her body swayed,
Knowing I was looking each step she did play,

Accentuating each movement as she slowly walked away.
A touch of her hand with skin so smooth
Sent the blood coursing, the heart began to move
A thump against the chest, now never to rest

How I long for the warmth of her hand upon my breast.
Her ghost still surrounds me, like a parcel of mist
Curls around my body, on my cheek leaves a gentle kiss
The picture in my mind never dull always clear

Shows the sparkle of her mischief, the joyousness sincere.
Stolen glimpses as she glided by, turning her head, pretending to be shy
Who was the hunter who was the prey, eyes so bright like a fawn did she play
A look, a smile, come hither her lips seemed to call

Like a rabbit in headlights I seemed to freeze and to fall.
The captured moments fleetingly pass, empty arms thin air clasp,
Her body close, I felt her within, moments of happiness I felt at last
How can a memory hold such pain, takes all the sunshine leaves only the rain?

A New Day

As the rain steadily falls and washes away the dirt of the day
A splash of a footfall in a puddle causes a ripple of movement
Yet the ripple has a short life span, as it reaches the edge it dies,
The force of its life's movement no longer there.

The clock will forever tick as it draws a life from one day onwards
We notice not this passing; we fail to plan on how to use this day
Too late we awake to find it gone, forgetting we are getting older
On borrowed time we laze about not knowing which direction.

The mirror reflects our image, yet our eyes will only see
The face of yesteryear of how we used to be
The brain refuses to acknowledge that time cannot stop
Yet we remain in the time of our youth, young and carefree.

As the bright light creeps through the curtains, the dawn of a new day
You pull the covers closer to your chin
Knowing deep inside you that the nurse will soon be here
Helping you to your functions in the now familiar way,

Oh where did the time go, it seems that not long ago
You were skipping down the high street, and playing in the snow.

A New Spring

Oh! I know now that which I seek, the quietness of a loving soul,
A smile that warms me to the core leaves a tingle in my fingers,
Have the wings of a dove so I could fly high carrying my true love.
To follow the flight of cupids arrow straight to your heart enfold.

Where my mind seeks tranquil peace and a cloud to rest my head.
As the clear blue sky rests gently upon the crest of a sea wave.
Each gust of warm wind to caress my face longs for the touch that I crave,
When the wisp of each cloud is changed into the picture that only I fleetingly read.

Where distance is measured in time and emptiness follows in line behind,
Should a heart grow cold and contrite, when dark and lonely is the night?
A hollow shell where emotions used to be, all drained of the spirit now taken flight.
Yet like the Phoenix rise from the ashes, be re-kindled to grow love once more in time.

A Passage of Time

Softly and gentle as a summer cloud
A whisper comes to mind
An echo of a memory not lost, just found
Captured from a time so long, long ago.

Like a favourite tune comes into the head
Soothes the body calms it instead
Leaves a smile, instead of a frown
A beam of happiness reaches the soul

Evokes a peace of all words said.
As the mind soars away escapes all earthly woes
While the spirit searches for the inner glow
Should the eyes imagine an angel only for you to know?

Allows the joy of expectations brings hope, to let this grow.
As a warm sensuous sea breeze caress the skin
While the sound of the sea waves kissing the shore
From a passage of time of which you are not sure

Where just one set of footprints traced in the sand
Asks who is there to guide and to hold firmly your hand?
For spring is the season to bring in new love
Where the days seem much brighter due to the sun

And passions grow stronger from being in love
Why then does heartache seem to follow each one?
Should a raindrop gently spatter the face?
If a distant rumble of thunder hurry your pace

If the leaves in the trees rustle out loud
As darkness descends due to the blackening cloud
Smile to yourself, don't be afraid,
Having fear is no disgrace

A Passing Gift

Give a little bit of Christmas just by making a present out of a smile
Make a strangers day, perhaps they are lonely or down for awhile,
It's just a simple but brief thing to show kindness still exists
The rarity of the moment changes a sad day to one of pleasurable bliss.

We humans are a funny race, pretend what we are not put on the airs and graces
It's all about impressing someone else, trying to stay in the races.
Although being normal doesn't always seem to fit into the vogue
It really could be great fun staying outside and being for once, the rogue.

Handing out this simple salutation can perhaps offer others a salvation
To alleviate the pressures bring a little sanity into their situation.
Just like the Christmas parcel wrapped for the special occasion
The passing gift you bestowed is accepted without any persuasions.

A Sad Farewell

Goodnight dear sweetheart of mine
Until next time our arms do entwine
The moment of bliss of your sweet kiss
Will burn in my memory for all time

The joys and good times we both shared
To others it showed that we truly cared
At moments like this how I needed your kiss
To settle my thoughts of you those that I miss.

How do I say a last goodbye to you?
From far away where I do stand, lonely too
Where a teardrop shall fall when I hear you call
From deep inside my head that is all.

If your last thoughts of me were of love
So deeply entrenched from above
Then my heart will abide as it bursts with pride
Thinking of the times when we both laughed and cried.

With your hand warm and tender in mine
And the shine of true love in your eyes
Your smile made my day as I longed for you to stay
Now the emptiness clings to me like a dampness of clay.

So goodbye to you my dear true love
Those many miles and years do us part
But my memories live on though my hope has long gone
Forever you will remain deep in my heart.

A Sweet Encounter

Have you not heard from the hum in the humbug?
Or tasted the butter in the butterscotch,
Now where is the money from the mint imperials?
Or got drunk on the wine from the wine gums.

Landed on the planet loaded with bars of mars.
Found or lost a fortune sailing on the good ship bounty.
Have you soared high into the dark empty void of the galaxy?
Or laid snuggled up on the hearth rug with your *Kit-e-Kat?

Have the children been kept quiet with the gobstopper,
While living on the posh confines named quality street
Or have you won an award which led to the celebrations
Where you and your friends were treated as heroes?

Did you hear the snickers coming from the minstrels
As you collected the posies of roses thrown by the fans?
Was the double decker enough to transport the revelers
Along the gravelled surfaced works road which was rather crunchie

All the way to the yorkie hotel?
Before returning for retirement, to the werthers original place of home sweet home.

A Walk Through Life

The spirits follow us everywhere though they can't be seen
Guiding and protecting yet sometimes this does not so seem
Each step we take is no mistake for eternity we are bound
Trials and tribulations in life, all of these are to be found.

Eternity is forever, especially when you are so young
To form and shape the character the process is prolonged
From babes in arms to boundless youth the transfer takes so long
The path through life is never lonely, just like the song that's sung.

At night whilst in slumber recharging every cell
The spirit watches over you to make sure all is well,
From young to middle aged to someone dear and very old
Each step along the path you trod you were doing as you were told.

For those whose time on earth is over, the spirit drifts away
So silently and quietly you join them on perhaps this your final day,
A smile of pleasure spreads across your face at the things that you have seen
You came into the world pure and unsullied; did you leave it just as clean?

A Warm Welcome

Just the old and battered lamp, sitting on the table
Casting moving shadows across the empty room,
The flames flicker noisily and hungrily in the fire place gable
Whilst the logs fizzle and crackle awaiting the family to come home soon.

Outside the winter wind blows leaving frost upon the window pane
Crunching of footsteps upon the crisp and freshly fallen snow
All noises are now softened like heat that eases the pain
The crisp air carries laughter, squeals and giggles and inside there is a warming glow.

Although winter is harsh and bitter, it has a beauty all regal, like a throne
Emboldening Mother Natures scenery, a sculpture shinning ghostly all in white,
Children become architects and builders what they make they alone do own
From the freshness time and busy feet turn it to become all sullied, no longer bright.

The landscape is all different now; inside the forest all is quiet, silent like the night
Exhausted by their playing, thoughts turn to going home, sadness at leaving their
    creations outside all alone.
Soon memories of their inventions are like the snow, dissolved, entering the warm and
    cosy room more squeals of delight,
The old and battered lamp sitting on the table surrounded by freshly baked fruity
    scones.

A Wonderful Feeling

A tinkle of water over smooth pebbles flow
Making a life's blood from so long ago
Yet carries a picture of your sweet face
From mountains to valleys no shadows does it place

For yours is the face that helps brighten the sun
The beam of a smile enlightens everyone
The spray of the water so fresh and so clean
Drives away evil, leaves everything with a sheen.

Like a breath of fresh air you entered my life
Not causing a ripple, gently entered within
Left me quite wondering of where I have been?
Puzzled and confusing my mind is astray

If I am in yesteryear or am I in today?
Is this a feeling to last very long?
Of memories aplenty to make into a song?
Or is this a sadness that drains away good

And leaves you emotional and not understood?
If you are mixed up, flustered and queasy
Wondering if a decision will come easy
How do you think, rational or clear?

Or are your decisions clouded with fear?
To be strong is a weakness,
For your head can be unfair
Whilst your heart is beating

Yet you know it's sincere.
How do you tingle, fingers and toes?
Does the blood in your veins speedily flow?
Are you all nervous, get shortness of breath?
And sometimes when talking, simply forget?

A Wonderful Love

What can I offer you now my love now that time has stolen all our youth?
My once strong arms that held you close now barely hold my walking stick
Although I know your face so well the mistiness tries hard to hide the truth
Where once I heard your step so clear, now sometimes I hear the awful click.

The time span that we have shared in love, the family grown and fled the nest
How sweet the times we knew so well how sad some tales we have to tell
With ups and downs that life did lead wonders how our love did survive the test
We have grown together from youth to age and all that time with you in love I fell.

With your skirts a billowing and your laughter echoing how good love did feel
Twirling around a dance floor the youthful vigour and great exuberance showed.
Though our youth was there once upon the time careful planning was not for real
Children arrived to great delight though in pregnancy I confess, you always glowed.

Our strength was in each others arms, your decisions final despite my choice
Hand in hand or arm in arm you would always lend to others some of your charm,
Folks adored you just as I, each anniversary passed and we did so rejoice
The aging process did not dim the joy of living even in bad health we both kept calm.

My gallant days have waned and died yet my desire for you though has not expired
Just getting old does frustrate and dull all functions that I once took for granted
With faculties failing, limbs slightly weaker yet the torch I hold for you is still afire
Yes it has been a Wonderful Love being with you each day a new love has just started.

A Wrong Decision

A glimpse of someone you once knew
Where times were hard yet life was true
Each thought that one was always right
Mistakes were made there is no respite.

Consequences of that awful plight
A broken home, emptiness now no delight
A lonely void with room to spare
Now longing for someone to share.

How long can bitterness hold fast
Not moving on, staying in the past
Shall I now no longer look?
Let go of all those hands I once shook.

Strange paths that once well I knew
Old landmarks remain yet slowly I outgrew
The well known faces still remain in place
Each keeping the secrets of the everlasting disgrace.

Though time will never give you any grace
The shame on you will not be displaced
The burden you will forever bear
Until in time someone will show you that they care.

Twilight Thought

If my kiss could gently land upon your lips and taste the sweetness of your heart
If my hands could lovingly trace the contours of your face,
If I could drink greedily of your warm desire while holding you in my arms
If dark clouds should steal the sunlight my beacon you would be

The loving harbour of comfort and sanctuary is quietly waiting there for me.
Should I fail to capture the warmth of your smile?
Or miss the love that shines forth from your eyes
Overlook the shallow breathing as the stomach does a flip

Whilst the pulse suddenly races, in truth this is no trick
It is love that is stirring slowly and surely, on us it takes its grip.

Am I to Blame

Yes I know that I look funny, though really it's not my fault
My head seems too large for me you see, and my ears do stick out
I have to wear thick glasses to understand the words that I am taught
And sometimes it is rather difficult to hear all things so you have to shout.

It seems that I get picked upon because of my demeanour
Although it would be fair to say that my body does look far leaner,
With skinny arms small hands and legs that are long and all spindly
The other children seem to take their turns to force me into humility.

I cannot change in what I am for nature did for me all that it could
I have to stand up for myself as my parents told me that I should,
Though some days I seem to cry a lot at the jibes and scornful words
At night when alone in bed I dream that I am normal, and clean of this curse.

Each day I stop myself in asking of how of this I became
My family are all different for I am the odd one out
However, our home is a happy one where love is all about
So I ask myself the same old question, am I the one to blame?

Ambitions Path

Why do I steal words from all the others?
When inside I'm screaming out in pain
I should have recognised the feelings
It seems that I have no pity also have no shame.

How I stole a blank canvas and covered it with snow
With crystals all a glowing what did I really know?
Terracotta vases in the sunlight red beauty from the ground
Pebbles washed by raindrops nature's raw materials lying all around.

Recognising the failures yet failing to recognise each success
Striving for the unknown using all of that which is best
Burning of the candle illuminating sinews taut and stretched
Moving through the sands of time knowing there will be no rest.

Treading on the weak ones whilst climbing to the crest
Like the meteor streaking through the sky destroying all the rest
Harsh and cruel the actions let others feel all the pain
For success is the ambition financial wealth is the gain.

An Age Thing

The eyes are getting misty
And the knees are getting weak
While the skin is getting crinkly
Now the bones begin to creak.

The memory is not so sharp
Nor focused as it used to be
It would remember what happened yesteryear
But forgets what was had for tea.

The energy levels plummet
No strength to stir the pot
Sitting in the armchair
Once comfy now not a jot.

Staring out the window
To see life passing by
In silent desperation
One looks up to the deep blue sky.

A clouds drifts past silent on the wind
No whispers of far past memories
Yet still able to shed a tear
Down the furrowed cheek it falls

Not fast but oh so slow
Yet in the heart there is no sorrow
And like the sun, one begins to glow.
In the glow there is an inner beauty

Not visible to the naked eye
It goes everywhere with you
This often makes one happy
So good you have to sigh.

You wonder why you miss the youth
Now spent with such gay abandon
Of the passion that life still offered
The pleasures of the four seasons.

The blame is placed firmly on the mind
If things should go astray
How cruel then we are to ourselves
Where it is age that this should lay.

An Awakening

Should the pace of life become a burden and a haven should you seek?
Over here stands a stranger, a new friend you should meet.
Comfort and safety in abundance, and a welcome here you could share
The hand of friendship beckons, the door remains open to show you that I care.

Oh heart, beat a little slower; eyes, clear from being blurred and bored
Let the pulse no longer race while the blood flow at a slower pace,
The roaring in the ears subside, tender be the touch as our hands embrace
Two minds are born of one accord the elixir of joy, bountiful will be our reward.

Would I be able to shrink the world, or make the sea a paddling pool?
One step across a continent would then seem not too far.
If I were able to reach into the night sky and thereby steal a star
Should I have to hold high the arch of the rainbow, or bow down to the rule?

Should a strong wind make you stoop, while wishing that the rain would cease,
If dark clouds hover overhead, what thoughts are stuck inside your head?
Just around the corner courage is found, new hope and faith is your new peace
The seasons now begin to flow, time for new deeds and honest words to be said.

An Empty Eulogy

Did I hear a whisper, or was it just the wind
How did I miss the broadest smile as you passed me by?
A swish of the skirt, a sway of the hips, tantalising tempting a sin
Follow a feeling indulge in the pleasure, once taken you cannot rescind.

An early morning greeting, I like the new style of hair
A blush, a quiet thank you, and then you are gone no longer there.
Passage of time turns slowly before I see you again
Those eyes and lips are calling come where I can touch you

The message seems to say, yet rooted to the spot, steadfastly I remain.
Do you have a favourite perfume; you see I'm not quite too sure
Yet stylish clothes you wear, so prim, neat and full of poise
Is there an Achilles heel with you, or has nature in you endowed

An elegance, or is it pure natural charisma that we see in the raw?
In reading peoples body language, on that I do not highly score
Into one thing I read another the minuses are a positive,
Or is it the other way around you see I'm still not too sure

Yet in my eyes you will always to me remain,
The beauty to capture attention when through my door you came.

An Ode to

With fag ash and lime
And old father time
Retirement is just over the hill
If you really don't know I think

I can show, for you there is a pill.
It rejuvenates bones, stops
Aches pains and moans even
Eases all creaks and woes

So a toast will be raised
To ring out and praise
A tipple that you will replenish
A celebratory clink

Of a nice healthy drink
From China or Ceylon
With it's refreshing taste
With you there is no waste

So here's Cheers to a nice cup of tea.

Another Day Thrown Away

Did you stop and stare only the other day?
For I saw a glimpse of someone I thought I knew
But the mind plays tricks and the eyes can misconstrue
For the fleeting shadow passed with no intention to stay.

As time and distance grew new thoughts began to bloom
The visions of the years to come, they can't be here it is far too soon
Yet cherish time as well we know, that once it's gone you cannot dwell
Each breathe we take is free for life, only in death we last expel.

While in youth time lingers as a dream untouched by human hand
Sparse thoughts of tomorrows, happiness or even sorrows
Take the moment enjoy it well, today is yours build castles of sand
As each grain through fingers flow, no more time can you borrow.

Looking back at all the days, what was ventured what was gained?
A blank canvas was there for you, to paint the dream you wished to come true
The brush is dry, no paint was used, no vision born, what did you do?
Just another day thrown away no sun was here on the day that it rained.

Captured Sadness

The picture hangs at an angle for the ghost of bad luck to slide off,'
Under the sullied glass the backing seems like canvas instead it is of cloth.
A captured childish innocence that has travelled well through time
Yet seeing the reflection no longer mirrored to the definitive line.

The gentle shy smile captivates and holds onto the beholder
Whilst eyes do follow and fears those slow and ponderous steps,
The sadness within the picture hides the child's wish to grow older
For when the painting was being done it was the time for regrets.

The cold and draughty garret with the naked bulb for light
She sits still for endless hours even shivering through the night,
Each brush stroke is a torment as the colours fail to blend
The smile is frozen to the face now, no loving message does it send.

With dry sightless eyes and lips now of the sombre blue
The skin is taut and cold yet still the artist to his labour remains true,
Forever now in silence within the painting her life is caught
Watching all who spy her, through endless time it is thought.

Castles of Sand

The sand upon your feet brought tears to your eyes
Not the heat nor the sea or the salt spray,
No comfort could we give you there was no disguise
The sand you did not like so you would not play.

Then a young lady arrived and you took to her brightness
Ran over the hot sand to her in obvious delight
In her arms you did hug, giggles of laughter rang out loud
You loved that day as a memory had been found.

Memories are built firm, not like castles of sand
Something to hold onto, to keep in your hand.
Eyes closed tight, think deep, this memory I will keep,
You can bring to life in dreams as you sleep.

Caught Off Balance

In a vacuum of time you are in limbo with a numb mind
Not knowing where you stand or why life's turned so unkind,
Offered to you was the saving grace by a tender loving face
With a happy heart on paper your soul wrote words at an endless pace.

The empty silence since now rests heavy upon your head
Each passing day is fearfully dread those words that were never said
One wonders how emotions can be awoken stirred then cast aside
For each word written was with feeling not a single one was a lie.

Her face appears before you with a radiant smile, bright her eyes do shine
How taunting the moist lips seem to be, tantalizing and yet so divine
Drifting silently away from you no footfall sound could be heard
Stealing the heartfelt feelings aroused by her into the snare I was lured.

The mind cries out in anguish the heart beats with the pain
The longing to be held by her, to feel her kisses sweet again and again,
Yet still her face remains before you while loving words yearn to be said
Not knowing where to turn too, caught off balance is she here or has she fled?

Childish Insistence

Why hide your face inside a bonnet does it cover the crimson blush?
Your hands, why do they tremble as the flower you hold, the petals you do crush
Why do your eyes flutter so when the man you behold is within your gaze?
Are these a sign of emotions stirring or simply a childish faze?

We hear the squeals and giggles shared amongst you laughing girls,
Yet we fail to understand what you are saying the words are stolen by the wind that
    gusts and swirls,
You point and tease even call his name more frequently, he, embarrassed standing
    within a crowd;
Ignoring his embarrassment persistent ever more, you call out again and rather loud.

Instead of getting angry the man of your insistence smiles and comes towards you
The bonnet has now moved, it is covering your sobbing reddening, tear stained face,
Two hands reach down and straighten this, the crying stops now you are so very glad
Planted kisses upon your cheek from the man of your bonded love, your own loveable
    Dad.

Circle

When the piano chord hits middle "C"
And the scale of music sets you free
More graceful as a butterfly be
When cobbled boots around ankles tied

As sweat and toil no longer counts
And harsh reality is what life's all about.
Where once a head was tilted up
To search for the buttercup

How shadows loom to destroy the light
And like a child, hate the night.
And in the meadow not yet shorn
Where ears of corn the rain does sup

The smells of sodden earth spew forth
Life renews bursts forth with glee
The circle of life, an anniversary.

Consider for a Moment

Who stooped on the beach to clasp the pebbles bright?
Straddled mountains, held head in clouds out of sight
Walked upon the ocean floor, sat upon the crescent moon,
Who pondered over this and that, decisions sought through the gloom.

Sat by a bramble bush to see the spider spin its web
Watched armies battle hard, caused rain to fall over tears they shed,
The distant rumble within the head pain felt as blood was spied
Anguish, sorrow all heartache felt watching as the whole world cried.

Nobody yet everybody creates and later in time then destroys,
The spiralling vacuum sucks out air then discards all like broken toys.
Through all this fantasy and idealism strive to exist side by side
Up to and beyond the point where mental worlds will collide.

The broken shattered pieces now lay strewn about
The collectors broom has since passed over there is no doubt;
Heavy swells borne of the strengthened and turbulent sea,
Pauses to consider the judgement of the planet and humanity.

Crystal Chandelier

How close to beauty do we stand yet blind in eye to see?
Each image set before us shapes heights or the depth of the sea.
Whilst dark heavy laden clouds clumsily drift across the sky
Casting shadows from each object as silently they pass by.

Yet out of nature, hewn from the eons of time
The fabric of our being our heritage our umbilical line.
History is red, steeped from battlefields soaked in blood,
Bright summer colours can be wiped out by the eclipse of the sun.

A piece of smoked glass throws out prisms when looking at the sun.
While the crystal chandelier sprinkles beauty that dances free with fun.
The golden orb of sunshine opens colours like the birth of the flower
As the clouds release its rain mother earth is thirstily waiting to devour.

The evolution of life is a circle that is spun in its own time
The journey of emotions like a cyclone never in a straight line;
Swept away with feelings at the once great beauty that used to be
Only devastation, chaos colourless and darkness is all that is left to see.

Destiny or Choice?

Sadly as the wheel of life swiftly turns and our life is unfulfilled
As our thoughts turn to yesterday and the opportunities overlooked
Taking only half the chances, ending up through life unskilled
Always looking on with envy at those who studied hard with the book.

The dream is not a vision just the flimsy plans fixed firmly within your head
Of how your life has panned out no fame, fortune or glory, just the shame instead
Every passing day gets harder to eke out each meagre coin of the realm
Seeing how the money pile is dwindling, knowing it was you at the helm.

Steering your path through the walks of life choosing what to do
Now at the wrong end of the spectrum, you've peaked now down the hill you slide
The spirits used to guide you, now abandoned, alone you know that you are through
In the twilight years of your short time here, carrying shame and embarrassment no
    longer can you hide.

Nowhere now left to turn too, no more callers at your door
Living in the shoe box blank walls show the future and what there is in store,
Had you worked hard in your younger years how clever now could you be
The question asked so many times, did fate have this ready waiting there for me?

Dragonfly

A Dragonfly came bearing a role with many a name
Of all the young children this disease would eventually claim
Why do they perish after suffering all of that pain?
Yet they all die with dignity, smiling bearing no shame.

Some stop their treatment to enjoy what's left of their young life
Giving pleasure to others, brothers, sisters husbands and wife,
In foregoing their treatment their death is assured
Though for them a smile of kindness is worth more than the cure.

Billions are spent on a rocket to Mars
While treatment for cancer, time and distance remain far
They fine you for parking on their hospital plot
Where this money goes –to patients not one single drop.

While a child on her death bed starts a Charity appeal for help
The hospital chiefs tell the nurses to tighten their belts
Rely on the funds to assist in their cause
The deaths of our children, this government refuses to give cause.

We care for our children in sickness and in health
Not knowing if the grim reaper will enter with stealth
We hope and we pray that our offspring are healthy and fine
Though become frightened and shattered if in illness their health would decline.

Now that it's done and they have passed on their way
Upon leaving a memory forever with you it will stay
A photo or movie something to hold onto so dear
While the disease that killed them, no miracle cure for others is near.

Ebbing Away

Trace a fingertip along the sand,
Taste the sea salt upon your lips,
Feel the warm breeze caress your skin,
Hear the gentle swish of the waves upon the shore

Gently close your eyes dream you're in another land.
The warm water laps at your feet as you walk along the shore
Hear the laughter of the children their squeals of delight.
See the dinghy boats bobbing across the ocean so light

Their whitened sails dance and dazzle in the sun
Everything is so perfect everything around is so pure.
Open your eyes and the darkness and dampness still clings
Like an overcoat sodden with water hard to shake off

You didn't escape as you planned, to get away from there
Struggle as you want to, does anybody really care?
Who can you turn to in your hours of need?
Who will help to care for you now that you are old?

In younger life you gave it all and let others share
Never dreaming in the twilight years you'd be turned out in the cold,
In higher circles its called progress, to others it is greed.
The sea sucks the sand from your feet and slowly you sink will no-one try to hear your
    despairing silent cry?

As the sun sinks over the horizon and the heat of the day ebbs away,
Alone on the beach, alone on the brink.
The seagull has sounded a last eerie call
Nobodies there to see your undignified fall,
While the sea salt has left you all sticky now
The breeze no longer warming, it chills upon the skin,
The sands of time are running out, is now alright to give in?

Eulogy for a Beautiful Stranger

How lonely does the heart beat when you're not there
Yet comfort is just a glance away at photo's one must stare
A warming feeling within one's self, gentle rhythm courses through
Little that you know of me though fate together, you and I threw.

My words stem from deep within as only true love does allow
The kindred warming of our being that is where these feelings dwell
In reaching out my hands to you when fingers gently touch
The feeling of reaching home is comfort and safety enough.

When moist eyes shine and the heart beats that much harder,
As the mind strives to understand the emotions of this ardour
How walking upon the empty air with head amongst the clouds
How thoughts turn to happiness when shrugging off dark shrouds.

So shed those tears of joyousness tell everyone you hold so dear
Explain that your time is now to share in the happiness,
Each day you count on numb fingers as your big day draws ever near
Joining in the union your whole being will hold forever and lovingly caress.

Every Second Counts

Tick-Tock Tick-Tock
I really cannot stay,
Tick-Tock Tick-Tock
I must be on my way.

Don't have time for this and that,
Don't have time to stop and chat
There are always things for me to do -
I really don't have time for you.

Tick-Tock Tick-Tock
I must be on my way
I just don't have the time to stay
If I stopped and talked to you

The time would simply slip away.
Tick-Tock Tick-Tock
I really cannot dally
We have another meeting rally

Targets set for me to achieve
I just don't have the time to breathe
Tick-Tock Tick-Tock
Oh yes! I really do like my job

The truth is and I cannot fob
The workload somehow increases
My nerves are shattered, I'm now in pieces
Tick-Tock Tick-Tock

Have I just arrived, or am I leaving?
Against the clock, it's so deceiving
The second hand is always clicking
The sands of time are forever seeping

Oh! Will that clock never ever stop?

Failing to Plan

Whilst in my youth it is very fair to say
Planning for the future was so far, far away
Not realising in truth of how handsome I did look
Fame and future fortune was easily overlooked.

Today I see film stars with far less sex appeal
If stood by me they would lose all they thought was real.
My panache and charisma would clearly shine through
No botox or face lifts, on me, all is still true.

Do you think that I am angry or maybe a little bit hurt?
Yet my body was honed my pecks taut when I took off my shirt
Before they were called as this I had a six pack so firm
All due to a medicine ball dropped to see if I would squirm.

In time their faces and neck lifts will eventually collapse
Furrows not wrinkles and the wearing of the neck cravat.
To apply tons of makeup and expensive facial cream
Intending to hide the ugliness that will leave them so obscene.

Now fame and fortune have sadly passed beyond my way
Yet I retain my good looks that god gave me on my birthday
With a straight back still and just the slight sign of a bulge
An evening out with friends at a restaurant I can indulge.

There is no such clamour for my autograph it is sad to say
No rolls or a Chevy no expensive toys with which I can play
A small two storey terraced house is all that I am worth
But I am happy with myself because quite simply, I'm on God's earth.

Feelings

When a person's feelings
Are all too easy to show
In the face and the eyes
They either dim or they glow.

All true feelings
Will show upon the face
Yet we try to immerse them
To save us from disgrace.

Just how did a heartbeat
Cause so much pain?
There is nothing tangible, just solid pain.
How the mind and the heart

In two separate parts
Can cause so much confusion
Sorrow and shame.
Shock to the system

Words spoken in truth
When someone is happy
In the decisions that they make.
A dew drop of pleasure

A fragrance oh so pure
The tread of a footstep
Will tell them you are near.
The glories of the sun's rays

Shone through the darkened clouds
The strength of a spider's web
Like the fineness of pure silk.
How nature is so gentle

Defined and surreal
The wonderful four seasons
We try to capture or attempt to steal.
The crispness of the snow

With the brilliance so sharp
How nature is so lovely
Our breath this comes in gasps.

Had

This word is quite emotive, sometimes of good sometimes of bad,
Tries to describe the feelings of those that we have had,
Remember the secret, rendezvous if only you had,
A special occasion, you wish that you had.

The occasions you didn't stand up for yourself, if only you had
The times you didn't keep your mouth shut, if only you had
Those times when you didn't turn the other cheek, if only you had
The diets you start and never kept to, if only you had

You never seem to under-spend, yet, if only you had,
You failed to go to a family gathering, if only you had,
The money you never seem to save, oh! if only you had,
Right place, but again the wrong moment, if only you had.

Missed opportunities because of bad timings, if only you had,
Lost moments of passion due to shyness, if only you had,
All those lost hours of your time, if only you had ,
Raised voices when silence would be quite right, if only you had.

Pushing and shoving to get to the top, if only you had,
Being quiet and reserved at the right time, if only you had,
Didn't recognise the right people, if only you had,
Didn't apply pressure at the right place, if only you had.

It's only at times like this that we realise that in truth, we have been well and truly
    HAD.

Half a Chance

Meeting at the bottom of a staircase
An uninspired venue of choice
An exchange of opinions something to voice
A cycle of events now set in place

Inexorably growing, gathering pace.
Darkness and gloom, drab and contrite
Step a little closer look deep into the light
For there is a brightness burning so fierce

It's angry and hungry, your drabness it will pierce
A furnace of heat your dampness it will defeat.
Like the whisper carried swiftly on the wind
You entered my life, smoothly as a ripple from a raindrop

Creating the arc of the rainbow so gently bowed
A warming caress upon me you kindly bestowed.
The lilt of the flute or the hum of the harp
Accentuates the senses, louder beats the heart

Listen out for the moment, be alert and be sharp
Consequences are severe as happiness is at stake
Miss and receive just half a chance, less reward to take.

High but not so Mighty

A tingle of anticipation the heartbeat more pronounced
In sudden realisation of what is soon to be announced,
As the mind is all swirling and the palms begin to sweat
No mumbles or fumbles the words spoken all must accept.

A dawning of understanding at the magnitude of the task,
Yet dreading silent moments before the questions they will ask.
No manner of teaching has prepared one for a situation like this
The swallows are much faster now; even worse one has dry lips.

How hard is life yet one has to expect grown ups to never falter
Although it would be fair to say they haven't faced my daughters,
One simple little question graced with eyes bright that do attract
Please Dad, dear Dad; can we have a lovely, lovely kitten cat?

Hoar Frost

How white is the day as the hoar frost has its way
Each branch of the tree outlined so crispy white
So cold is the day birds have all flown away,
No sunshine can seep through to give us delight.

With topcoat and mufflers and wearing mittens too,
Each breath taken as sharp as the pin exhaled air as a bubble of smoke.
Icy paths trodden with a careful tread, searching for footsteps to follow through
Balancing precariously, sometimes on one shoe, nothing seen, no words were spoke.

A swish of noise as a car flashes by icy cold wind is their farewell sigh
Eyelashes heavy now laden with frost, vision impaired caution is lost
More haste is given as the shops do appear the flashing beacon is now close by
Almost there with eyes squinting tight to get the shopping done whatever the cost.

Now laden with bags in either hand the balance is better, you understand,
Returning more slowly across the icy paths slipping and sliding, twirling around
A nasty thump as one falls in a heap, shopping bags scattered all over the ground
The frost is quite chilly as it seeps into the skin, where is somebody? you need a hand.

What is the time you suddenly ask/ dawning now the size of your task
The coat you are wearing is so heavy and wet the shivers take over as you get cold
The frost is now so thick silence all around, what was the question you needed to ask?
Alone on the path nobody to help it is then that you realise you are getting quite old.

A squeal of delight as children find you whilst out at play
Not knowing your situation they begin to go on their way
The voice is now so very, very low you grab at something not letting go,
So help they gave and now your at home, snug and warm no longer alone
Looking out the window all crisp clean and white, instead of frost you prefer snow.

How Dark is Love

The first taste of love is sweet as honey
Each lingering kiss explodes in the brain
Dizzy and light headed, floating on air
No feat is unconquerable no sleep is divine.

Time flows and the passion once surging subsides,
Caresses once yearned for now turned away in spite
Gentle strokes of the fingers, loved beyond delight
Now resented forever as turned away in flight.

Love started together and went forging along
Overcoming all obstacles, not dallying too long
Sweet passion of time oh where did you go?
Alone and empty hearted again with nowhere to go.

In taking the love and all fervent passion too
The heart grows heavy not knowing what to do
In giving the sunshine and making the dream
Now left all in shadows, no hope to be seen

Is love everlasting in hearts that are true?
Yet the mind of the unfaithful plans what to do
By closing the curtains to the truth of true love
Brings deceit and great pain to those that were loved.

In return for the giving, in life as well as love
Not seeing the darkness clouding out the sun
Losing sight of the horizon, with nowhere to run
The haziness of the mind, the feeling of coming undone.

How strange that a feeling once joyfully held
Can be shaped into the weapon so eagerly used
To obtain material objects so easily obtained,
Yet love that is so fragile is treated with disdain.

So where do you travel in searching for true love?
How will it be recognised as the true and only one?
Will there be a fanfare with trumpets a blaring?
Or will it be silent, the one that is sharing and caring?

Oh shadows so dark and deeply buried inside thee
That makes the soul so cold, damp and unkindly
Disperse, break up and torment no more,
Leave quickly so the sun can once again warm the core.

The dark side of love gives suffering and pain
It sucks out the goodness without any shame
It clogs up the arteries, veins and the brain
Leaving the empty shell to draw life back into it again.

51

I Should Have Listened

I'm sorry Mum, I just did not listen to you I thought I knew best
Your advice just went over my head, I'm jack the lad I know the rest
Nineteen going on twenty five, drink and smoke sometimes take an upper
A bit of bother now and then not trouble really but I'll be home for supper.

I'm sorry Mum; I won't be home questions all about this and that
My mates have all legged it left me so I'm here to take all the flack
Didn't know he was in there when we torched the building just for fun
Fireworks display was brill, didn't hear the bill, but me mates just run.

I'm sorry Mum; it looks as though I'm here for more than a bit
Bad news I'm afraid things have just got worse the poor geezer's snuffed it.
If I grassed them up there would be a stink, they have mates inside doing a stretch
What do I do now Mum? It's not soft inside as shown by Porridge and Fletch.

I'm sorry Mum; it looks as though I'm going down for more than awhile
Why didn't you tell me about me mates Mum? You could have put me right
You never help me Mum, now I'm in trouble I have to face the court while on trial
Mum I'm scared, the days okay but I'm in a cell with other men all blooming night.

I'm sorry Mum; all the times you told me off I just thought you liked your own voice
I need your advice now Mum, I'm stuck in a small cell it's sad I don't have a choice
I miss my own room now Mum, and you and Dad, when you visit me I'll be so glad
Time does fly Mum, it's been a week now, and how much longer do I have to be bad?

I'm Asking for an Angel

Her picture, stuck up on the wallpaper with a blob of sticky blue tack,
Staring out from somewhere stretching deep into the void
Searching for a new love from a piece of celluloid
Hoping to find her soul mate and walk into a brighter future, never looking back.

There is no simple rhyme or reason to fall in love with a photograph
Perhaps it was her beauty, her smile or her eyes that cast the spell
Sadly though my feelings aren't mirrored and from the great height I fell,
With politeness and a kindness she gently placed me back upon the lonely path.

In hindsight I see the failing I had put my faith into the written word
Perhaps expecting a miracle that she would fall in love with the words that she heard
I could perhaps, be one of many to fall in love with her beautiful soft face
Her eyes do shine her lips entice to yield would somehow not be a disgrace.

Myself, I am no great picture although I've handled time with some success
I try to think of positive things so that I don't feel any of life's stress.
My search for love has widened now, it's to the skies I look I'm asking for an angel
For I thought I saw her aura as my spirits rose up high, before to the ground they fell.

Image

Hush, though we are still breathing
And our breath is shallow and dry
Vision is dancing like angels in the sky
Warm air is stirred by the vulture's wing.

With eyes dry, caked by the blowing sand
Throats parched through lack of water
Stumble along and reach out to clasp a hand
Shimmering image appears yet all are distorted.

Waves huge torrents of salt water crashes down
Feet cannot stand firm, no grip just slip from side to side
Hands wet not able to hold firmly, fall to the ground
Head gets banged, blackness, fall and slide and slide.

Icy cold numbs the body, white all around
Shivering and shaking, prisms explode in the head
Eyes scream as vision distorts, white from sky to ground
An image emerges, a huge white fur thing, warmth instead.

Noises beat the eardrums, smells evade the nose
Greyness cocoons you, softness underneath
Feeling of lightness floating feathers arose
A firm grip of the image, or the truth in belief?

Kamikaze

My words are humble as was my journey out of the night
I have seen what blind people will not see or ever suffer
The mist of darkness slowly drifting in to suffocate the light
I hear things that the deaf folk will be spared so cannot utter.

The coming of evil grows and pulsates within our midst,
I stood tall and wore pride glowing from my face
Love for the freedom of my country I couldn't disgrace
Now I sense the coming of darkness and that danger will persist.

From pre-historic man to cave man up to us, the modern man,
Each step advances in life and medicine gained, Homo sapiens future firmly laid
In life always a runt or a throw back is born, nature's method of cleansing is then
    displayed
As we have good so we also have bad, now the viper hides and will strike when he
    can.

Young men, not yet out of their teens fat around the waist looking obscene
Crowded tube stations death and destruction, young men no longer to be seen.
Old men gather to discuss events of the day, smoking and drinking, alive and well
The word martyr is praised and exulted, which part of a body was stuck to the shell?

History tells us of the Divine wind, those young men too did not want to die,
So please explain to me why the name martyr is used so much? it is quite inane
To believe in your faith* is the Godly thing, a martyr then you cannot be, or do you
    lie?
We read of your death only today, this time next week, who will remember your
    name?

Inside their homes our old people stay, in their lifetime it just wasn't this way
Peace and well-being, law abiding people was the order of the day.
Our country was united in a very special way, freedom of life with plenty of choice
Now multiculturalism has entered and this has slowly eroded the Englishman's voice.

I fear for my country and all Englishwomen and the men too
For a lawless state is coming and beckons earnestly to you,
Your time is over your rights have been amended and slowly taken away
History books will leave blank pages, as the obituary to this, the fateful day.

*Martyr, a person who is put to death for refusing to
    renounce a faith or belief, a person who suffers for
    adhering to a principle, cause etc, a person who suffers or
    pretends to suffer in order to obtain sympathy or pity. Put
    to death as a martyr, torment
Make a martyr of oneself, accept or pretend to accept
    unnecessary discomfort

Lover's Lament

I can only wonder at the beauty I behold
With sparkling eyes and glossy lips
The smile so full of loving
For me I wish to be told.

Hearts beat faster in the chest
Blood courses through the veins
Passion keeps on growing
Yet showing no sign of shame.

Each time my eyes look upon you
My heart gives such a leap
I swear one day I will end up in a heap,
Though I am never with you

The feelings will not subside
I need you to be, forever by my side.
Your face is always with me
I smell your sweet perfume

Although I cannot touch you
You are always in my dreams.
Sweet lady of grace, please do not displace
This hopeless love of mine

Spare a look a glance so swift
A mere mortal can hold so dear
The spirits lift and life goes on
With a dream that is so sincere.

Lucky Us

Does the horseshoe really hold in all of our luck?
In our search for this is it the four leaf clover that we pluck?
Is there always to be a pot of gold at the end of the rainbow?
Calling a double- headed penny lucky, this just cannot be so!

Perhaps we'll get lucky doing the national lottery one night
Failing that there's the horses or dogs even bingo to give us the bite,
There is also a scratch card for a quick rub, or a newspaper to give us a lift
Doing a comp is great for the soul because a freebie holiday is a great gift.

Throwing coins in a fountain, or down the wishing well
A dream of winning great fortunes always makes us feel swell.
But the dream disappears as there are no lucky numbers this Saturday night
Enter another comp everything's fine and the luck will work out all right.

So when we pass over do we really go up into heaven?
Shall our spirits flow through time and space but at the gates remain?
Shall the milky- way hold us to her bosom our illusions to daze?
Will our souls become the future twinkling stars for others to gaze?

Misinterpret

It wasn't a dream then, I did feel your warm cheek
It was your sweet spell that I came under?
When you held me it was that as a lover not as a friend
Reluctant to let go yet too shy to remain close to me.

Shall I remain a mortal or will I walk among the Gods?
Should I serve a penance for daring to embrace you?
Yet it was you who intoxicated me, first with your smile
Then your dark eyes flashing, the aloofness drove me to distraction

Longing to talk to you yet your distance did you stay?
My ears still ring with your spoken words
You pop into my thoughts without warning
My eyes see you though you escape my arms

Have you now walked out of my life not wishing to stay?
How thoughts can turn to desire at a simple whim
How body language miss-read turns into a sin
How the longing to drink from the loving cup is forbidden from within

Shall the hunger for completeness disappear in the wind?
The fragrance of your perfume lingers around my head
Your smooth silky skin left the kiss of longing upon my cheek
Should a promise be forthcoming needless I would stay

Feeling completeness I wonder just what you would say.

My Elfin Mirage

Too swift the moment passes each time I close my eyes.
How loud and fast the heart beats when close to you I stand
Eager is the passion inside of me waiting to be released
Yet in distance you do stay, forgoing all the pleasures for another day.

Fool that I am, I had the chance to ask of you
One date to see if we too each other would be true.
Wasted chances though time does not allow
For neither distance nor empty lives does sow.

Imagine rain without a puddle or snow without the cold
How the sun can change a rainbow but never change the soul
A solemn cloud wraps around me as you pass out the door
How long before I see you if I can ask of more?

As nervous as a kitten who's seen an elf just once
Not knowing the way forward, brave heart it must trust
What would be the outcome, if there is a time for us?
Do we play the waiting game or act upon a hunch?

Small neat and yet so petite my elfin mirage dream
Never have I seen you look more beautiful
Nor so joyously warm the smile from you I've seen
Your eyes shone so brightly little could they disguise

The happiness inside of you for your eyes told me no lies.
How my blood flowed faster as side by side we stood
So much I have missed you, a glimpse, a smile, a touch
If only for a moment a tender kiss I could steal

My feelings would be found out, false or are they real?
Yet deep within my heart the hunger sought of you
Burns a desire of belonging, only to you it must be true
Awake or asleep you are with me always on my mind

Your face is my comfort my joy and inspiration too
Your warmth my inner glow, your heart if dreams come true.
Like the willow you are so sleek and slender
The inner strength you do well to conceal

Hiding inside your emotions, not showing how you really feel
If only I could render the love you so desire
For your loving beauty will blossom the real you it will reveal.
Should I be so lucky as to receive that tender kiss?

The momentary pleasure will last a lifetime of bliss
The beautiful fleeting treasure will give me happiness
To linger in my memory, to be restored by just a wish.

My Lovable Ghost

In truth inside me is where I miss you the most
A calming influence, a heartbeat my lovable ghost
My guide and protector my shelter my strength
To keep you beside me I will go to any length.

The colour green is soon dispersed to a calmer hue
Should an irritant arise you will always come through
You're not a spirit just pure flesh and blood
Someone to see, hear, hold onto and to love.

You are with me each step of the way
Although we are strangers I would like you to stay
For our destinies were planned long, long ago
By someone greater who loves and cherishes you so.

On the day of your birth I cried out with joy
A child full of beauty and grace no one could destroy
The warmth you gave as I held you close
At that one moment in time I loved you the most.

I carry you with me now on my long lonely walk
Should I ever need a friend, it is to you that I talk
I hear an echo of your laughter, see your happy smile
If time would allow I would stay for more than a while.

New Feelings

Should our lives suddenly become entwined, and our hands gently touch
Would a tender glance be just far too much?
Should the pulse suddenly race fast and hot?
Could it be that a look would be forgot?

Are we to old to wish upon a star?
Should we stop and wonder where we are
While the music still warms and stirs the heart
Reminding us of its important part.

Rhythms and beats, it moves both hands and feet
Slowly, gently it creeps into your soul
Awaking the feelings that grief once stole
Placing new memories, not bitter but oh so sweet.

In the early hours of the morning just as a new day is dawning
Where all is quiet and before all the yawning
Should you look up into the sky to see stars still shining?
And wonder why your heart is no longer pining?

Once Seen

As the mind grows dim with age and the eyes lose the lustre
The effort to stir a cup of tea with all the strength one can muster,
While the hearing is more distant now and the false teeth do click
Thoughts of all the yesterdays too swiftly through the mind they flit.

Why the passage of time erodes all the youthful vigour,
Although youngsters behind the backs do snigger
The changing world looks on with dissipation
Yet you know in your life there was some trepidation.

How now the sallow youth abandons life for debauchery
Drinking and bingeing, using drugs escaping real life with its sorcery,
Education spurned and respect not given now no longer valued
Random killings just for fun; kicking people until they are black and blue.

The veteran sits alone with thoughts of horror
Wishing that there would be no tomorrow
Shut away deep behind the eyes horrors seen cannot be disguised
Pals lost from a time long ago forever in the mind, reside.

Lost lives, good souls gone, sacrificed and for what?
Din and noise, blood and gore then silence as one gets shot.
The world's gone backwards to the feudal times
Standards and honour now belongs to book stories and nursery rhymes.

Open Philosophy

Let not the world surprise you, accept it with an open mind
With two feet firmly planted life will not brush you aside
A challenge is worth celebrating with the fortitude of kind
Enjoy the life's simple pleasures in the brotherhood of mankind.

Let the nobility live in all their splendour and put jealousy away
For all folk are equal given each their three score years and ten,
Nothing will ever change us, though astrologists try to make us sway
Believing in the function of dead planets, yet doubting the Chinese feng.

Seeing is believing stay focused on what is there
For the eyes do not deceive you reach out touch it if you dare.
That which nature gives us free surely is enough for all we really need
 Yet those made by man are done for exploitation, purely there for greed.

Our Flexible Finger

This special digit our favourite one
A mind of its own has all the fun
From eye to ear head and our bum
This finger without doubt is the special one.

It's always there it's in your face
Yet no-one treats it with distaste
The private parts has its allure
When no ones looking down it goes for the cure.

Around the back down to the bum
And the first one there for the rumble tum
Clean the belly button then have a scratch
Squeeze the boils ready for another batch.

From there it travels down to the toes
A rummage there before going up the nose
From Chimps to the upper echelons of life
Why even this finger works on the wife.

Crooked finger beckons a scratch or two
The worlds freedom digit points directly at you
Don't dare to stand there alone and in its way
Or the firm finger will be poking and prodding away.

Our Suffocation

Through our eyes, what do we see?
The beauty of nature, or mans catastrophe?
Where once nature's colours were as clear as our skin
Now darkened and sullen coloured by mans' sin.

Clear crystal waters and clean sweet purified air
Now poisoned by chemicals because nobody cares
The forests are devoured as we now need more space
For highways and byways and for skyscrapers disgrace.

Ciske

No ringlets of curls, no shimmering of the early sunlight
No golden rays of the bright burning sun
No dancing glimmer of misty halos as a new day is begun
No heavenly choir of angels as a new joy is within sight.

Dark tapering arches of the eyebrows
The soft fluttering of mascara laden eyelashes
Silhouetted against the creamy paleness of your face
The contours of your beauty my fingers want to trace.

Short dark hair snuggles against the nape of your neck
The dewdrop of your earlobes invitingly to kiss
Dark eyes smoulder above nostrils wide and flared
Challenging you neither to stumble nor to miss

The beauty and the pleasures of one sweet tender kiss.
Lips so full of promise, richness and tenderness too
Form above a delicate and determined chin
A throbbing pulse in the hollow of the throat

Words were formed within the head but the lips never spoke
Inside of ones head the senses begin to swim.
Through my ears I hear the lilting tone of your voice
 My minds eye still sees your beauty and your grace,

 Eyes shine with tenderness displayed without disgrace
The temptation of your lips, the softness of your smile
Could I only hope it is me that you wish to beguile?
Intoxicated forever by your beauty

Captured completely by your elfin charms
My salvation and my glory is found only within your arms.

Phoenix

Should we capture the secret of the chameleon?
Or of the ladybird as she spreads her wings
Try to bottle the freshness of the mountain spring air
Embrace the mysteries of the pharaoh's from another aeon.

Seek the pot of gold at the end of the rainbow
Or be like Icarus and fly up to the sun
How dark and light will shape and form us
A creation, unique, the sole and only one.

In searching out the mystic holy grail
In belief in our search we would not fail.
Longing just once to hold the golden cup
To place our lips where he once supped.

If love is eternal so pure and so divine,
Bringing the flush of youth to those old now in time.
Where here lay the ashes of a Phoenix instead
As young and in springtime where the sun now does shine
Reliving the moments, reclaimed from another lifetime.

Premeditation

A smile is the action a blush is the re-action
A stolen kiss that is worth the rebuke
Harmless actions that sometimes causes pain
Yet premeditation is always overlooked.

Everything is linked nothing is by chance
We think over our actions then do the deed
Whatever we do we hope to succeed
In life and for death people wear a mask.

Through life we have greed to reach to the top
We swindle and use others to get what we want
The piles of dead bodies litter our path
Only the best will survive to be the best of the crop.

If you're looking down from the pedestal so high
Is the price that you paid making you shy?
Premeditation is not too bad a word
If it is something you know of

Or quite simply what you have heard
It conjures up a medicine to ward off a cough.
Or of an old man taking his snuff
But used out of context, an evil it can be

Like planning a bad thing or taking a life
Or the disagreement between a husband and wife.
But what are the consequences should a leader of the land
Use the position and power to take away the medicine man

Is it premeditation or just another mystery that ended a life?
Perhaps then a simple way of navigating strife.
If one sees the truth and one sees the mirage of an oasis
One sees the grain of sand the other sees a speck of dust

Use of the duster is thought to be enough
As slowly as the moon does wane so too will the truth prevail
For hidden in the grain of sand is found the wrongdoer's hand.

Purity of Love

Left alone in slumber my dreams are of you
Fantasizing of our life together and the things that we need to do
How once, easily taken for granted to be used at others whim
Do you feel that this is the real thing pure and without sin?

Every fibre of my body yearns for your tender loving touch
Inside my heart beats wilder while my senses are reeling far too much
In dreams I find I have all control, I'm firm, loving and masterly too
Should I stand close beside you, I'd just wonder what I would really do.

From being starved of all loving feelings for many a long year
To think at last I have found true love fills me with wholesome cheer
Yet this is in my dreams alone real life leads on a different track
Lifts your spirits high one giddy moment then drops them down flat.

Though I often dream of you in purity alone
I hide my romantic feelings until I am at home
Here I hold you close to me and embrace you in my thoughts
For in reality I know that true love never runs the smoother course.

Question of Fate

O' Fortune of fate and man's desire let your rhythms dictate
While the heart does gently beat and the body perspires
The single whisper draws a man onwards to meet his fate
Yet womanly wiles drag hungrily and wantonly on all his desires.

Let the chaliced cup of love forever overflow the brim
Should empty arms in dismay yield to another source?
Whilst hunger for the warmth draw the light from the eyes to leave them dim
Then wonder why a true heart in pain does turn to take the other course.

If loneliness is simply the test of man to shape him in perfect stead
Surrounded by all he craves then temptation becomes his downfall
Who then will stand with open arms in welcome, or have they now fled?
Shall a man challenge temptation standing tall or on knees does he lowly crawl?

Are we moulded purely by ourselves or by some higher being?
Can the destiny be altered to that of what we yearn for and desire?
How do the celestial heavens look upon us without even seeing?
The hunger for companionship as man and woman does complete the human pyre.

Raindrops of Reason

The rain splatters upon the window pane
As the pulse of life you strive to contain,
Yet anger flows deep within the chest
The urge to hurt others you must confess.

Where within the heartbreak abides
Born from anguish, the deceit and lies;
Ostracised from those for whom you once cared
Forgotten now the life of which once we shared.

As years pass by the sadness you try to control
Though aid is not there any life line of which to hold.
A forced smile to greet a face a steady gait no hurrying pace
The bitter chill is on the wind now life is no longer a race.

Four seasons since have so swiftly come and gone
Inside the hollow feeling, yet somehow one must remain strong
Perhaps this is the trial one must have to suffer some of the pain
Regain all righteousness before wishing it would cease to rain.

Rear View Mirror

Just a piece of glass, polished to reflect
Vision from behind you showing what to expect
Rear seats, once occupied by my daughters two
Now are always empty the vision goes right through.

Each look into the mirror I expect fondly to see
Two little faces happily smiling cheekily back at me,
They never seem to age at all, still young and carefree
I wonder why I see them or is it really all in my memory?

Many cars I've had since the day I was faced with fear
Yet still I see them there, am I delusional or just a fool?
If so how then can I hear them their words are so clear
Encouraging me to go faster, yet I must remain in charge and cool.

Now my mirror is tilted up, no reflections do I see
The seats behind are now empty no longer carry precious company
How sad it is for a grown up to play at having a happy family
It's just me now driving on my own, remembering, living on my history.

Remember

I will always remember the way that she looked
The gleam in her eyes, the slight of her smile
The smell of her hair, the fragrance of her perfume.
Would my eyes ever leave her face as I gloried in her splendour?

So near yet so far, out of reach.
My heart is stricken as my blood flows hot
The temples hurt as the pain is shot.
Should I reach out and gently caress

Her sun tanned face that has been so blessed
Am I to be taunted, forever haunted?
She is there in the memory, awake or asleep
A face in the mirror, the warmth in the shower

Always around me or the face in street
Deep inside I know she has this power.
Should I approach her when she's not alone?

Responsibilities

The whispers were all silenced as into the room one strolled
All eyes turned downcast as past the throng one rolled
The feeling of expectation was following your every move
What demands now are called of this, calm waters must be soothed.

Now all eyes are upon you eager to watch the ungracious fall
Failing to understand that because of this one stands quite tall
Decisions' regarding each one of them to see if all bodes well
Though some must suffer because of failure to these one must tell.

Responsibilities on slim shoulders lay a fairness one must extol
No favourites or those close to you earn sanctuary from the final blow
Figures do not lie they say, those who have achieved therefore will stay
But ponder well on those who failed for tomorrow is another day.

Scar

Do I cry in hunger, or do I cry in pain?
Valiant in life what do I have to gain?
Scrambling along on fingertips who can complain?
Shredded into tatters where do I remain?

Harboured by the sea wall, splattered by the rain
Lost in all the darkness, no saviour can I name
Turbulent winds surround me forcing me on my way
Nowhere here to rest, nowhere here to stay.

Along with my own company in solitude I will stay.
Facing all the consequences of my actions along the way
Can it be wrong for me to burden all the guilt?
Yet have I the mental strength so that I will never wilt?

The raven flies overhead, the scar upon my cheek
A symbol for all to see that one time I was weak.
Night time darkness gathers and hides all the shame
Yet on a new day dawning, the shame will rise again.

Must we then hide or run away from life itself
Not searching out our special one, to remain in isolation
Closing doors behind us not seeking retribution
Walking on the lonely path is not the ideal solution.

Sharing

Hold out your hand and I'll gladly accept
Offer your friendship as a treasure it will be kept
Should I offer my feelings how would I fare?
How should one show to others how they care?

How I miss the sparkle in your eyes, the smile on your lips
The shake of your shoulders, the turn of your head as you pass by
The roll of your hips, the slow small steps when it is me that you spy
Am I reading too much that I want into this, do my eyes lie?

A wish was expressed, the desire shone through
All in confusion I missed out on the clue
I carry for you a torch that burns so bright
Inside my heart when I see you beats with delight.

Dear heart should your desires match mine
Should your inner self brightly shine?
Allow a message to come through telling me that it is I whom you choose
For I fear that it is you who should make the first move.

Days pass so swiftly and I know of the cost
You're a beautiful woman forever in my thoughts
Were I never to win you I would suffer pain of my loss
Time is against us, don't let us be distraught.

Shed one Single Teardrop

Shed one single teardrop
And deep inside thee stirs
A feeling so natural and wonderful to see
It stems from deep within the heart.

And shines right through the eyes
It lifts ones spirits up to the skies
It enables in us, all joys to be seen
A rarity of beauty within only thee

The flower is a thing of fragrance
Beauty and has the elegant grace
With velvet like petals and pollen sweet to taste
To drink from the nectar of that natural spring

Shows us to cherish all natural things
The dewdrop on the blade of grass
The drone of the humble bumble bee
 The chirp of the cricket, or the splash of the bass

As pollen silently drifts upon the soft dry winds
Nature leaves eyes so sore and nose running free
So drink of the nectar from life's giving cup
Mother Nature will feed us at her table she would like us to sup

Although caution must be taken not to strip everything bare
For mother nature cannot keep giving if the humans don't really care.

So Near yet so Far

Across the room your smile did bloom
Clearing the darkness dispersing the gloom
Your eyes shone bright my heart beat in delight
Your cheeks did glow with a crimson hue

Turning, you left leaving my being feeling blue
When our eyes did meet what message was sent?
Each second I watched you remain in my head
I know the words needed, which had to be said

Yet incoherent mumbles flowed forth instead
I have captured your smile in my minds eye
I've measured the heartbeats till we meet again
As a bee to a honey pot, so I'm drawn always to you

What surprises what pleasures if these feelings are true
It was felt I fear, as we stood near
That my desire would overtake me
In my arms I wanted to enfold you

Feel the warmth of your face upon mine
Such a wonderful feeling would be so divine
Although my head is strong, I feel the body is weak
The mind knows the words yet the voice does not speak

So near yet so far, I try to hold onto you close
In real terms of life I'm left clasping a ghost
Should I need to hang my head in shame?
As these thoughts of you in my head remain

If death is a release then torture is of being apart
Now confessions are needed you have stolen my heart.

The Bed

Where is the place of which we all adore, where sanctuary is always sought?
That which is craved for in our time of despair of where our peace is brought?
Often anger, rage and passion is fought over sometimes even death can be found
Yet for all these emotions we entrust each other and in this our spirits are bound.

A place we can curl up and forget all our woes, where we escape too nobody knows
It can be soft as the feather or as hard as the rock in times of distress we are all lost
To recharge our cells for our bodies to regain strength the need for this is heaven sent
We cannot malfunction in our daily chores for should this happen we must repent.

The place to escape when seeking our space in doing this we have ourselves to face
The haven of peace and solitude to cleanse our mind find our own space
Each shape that we form eases the pain allows us to focus without losing our way
Yet in slumber as a time cycle is spent, escape from reality yet longing there to stay.

The Calling

Lost in the vacuum of time, drifting like the desert sands
A closing of the mind from the offerings so divine
Rejecting the heart of someone who now can't understand
How the dreams which were so comfortable and sublime

Lie shattered and discarded, lost in the space of time.
A promise made on paper, thoughts from inside of the head
Words carried the dream for perhaps someone else instead
Now lonely and in limbo with a heart torn in shreds

Watching the world go by wondering which wrong words were said.
Two worlds have been changed by an expression of ones thoughts
Neither unkind or hurtful lost in translation true meaning never caught
How the restless soul is turning beckoned by a feeling calling one to home

The strong bond of mutual feelings forged whilst both were on their own.
The memory stores warm words deep within the head
Stirring the emotions somewhere deep inside the chest
Yet no tender touch was given no embrace or smile that misled
Just words upon a paper written as feelings or emotions flowed within the breast.

The Clarity of the Question

Ah, it was explained which was as clear as mud
Nothing but surprises or as helpful as chewing the cud,
But what was the question to bring about this response
Everything that harbours nothing yet holds the solution thus.

Standing by the waterfall and listening to the thoughts
Making sense of silence and the echo's of a sound
Upside down the world is as clouds come from the ground
Looking through the mist of spray at the temptation that it's brought.

Dark and damp as the coal mine suspended now here in space
The depths of eternity or the distance between each simple pace,
How solid clouds appear to be through an illusion of the minds eye
A fearsome furnace in the centre of the earth, is there a reason why?

The Empty Orchard

The sweet fragrance of the cherry blossoms have now sadly soured
Love that was slowly growing has turned inwards and been devoured,
Where once in pleasure I read your words now a emptiness fills my soul
The vanity I had within myself overpowered me, I lost sight of my goal.

In shadows now I linger, the orchard has lost all of its appeal
The fruit I once tasted is now bitter, there's dryness on the peel.
The sunlight slowly dims and behind the trees it now slumbers
Hidden from all prying eyes the mortal knows he split his life asunder.

In tasting the fruit from every tree greed and lust led to dishonesty,
Temptation beckoned from every branch driven on by an empty promise
Desire to sample fruit so rich and plump place one's lips on welcome flesh
The sin destroys all trust and hope the need to believe in truth is less.

Now upon the barren land naked of all its succulent splendour,
The empty orchard stands alone a constant painful reminder
Forbidden fruit tastes as sweet as honey it also sticks hard to the lips
Once smitten by these honey traps your sunlight sadly will be eclipsed.

The Eyes of Her Soul

Should the body yearn for a new love and life experience?
When from nowhere this apparition miraculously appears
How then do you know that she is the one to make your body cheer?
This surely is when the soul surrenders with little or no resistance.

Explain to me how the eyes from her photo captivate my being?
Ensnare and bewitch me to the subliminal weakness and hold my heart
Not one word has passed her lips yet the longing to be for her the matching part
The flush of love from her eyes the beaming smile upon our first seeing.

My heart travels many miles to find her smile united by an inner feeling
Comforted by her eyes welcomed by her hands and crimson upon her cheeks
This sudden burst of wanting, to let her know I'm true and not concealing
Strangers in the way of love afraid to offer more just yet until on this we've slept.

Though I love to look deep into your eyes there is stirring warmth inside
Emotions awake that have long since slept, the birth of love a heartfelt pride,
If truth and honour should prevail my conscious is clear for I will not fail
To win your hand, your heart your love my perseverance will prevail.

The Fragile Mind

Do I see you happy and content should we be together?
Will our lives entwine or will our time be short and spent?
Can a light of happiness shine bright through the darkness it rent?
Or for only a brief moment, sweet joy is just lent!

Do we chase the elusive dream or deep in shadows stay?
Should clouds have a silver lining, what price was there to pay?
Where there is hope and a story who will write the play?
Yet the joy in the heart a lifetime it will remain.

If time were a passion how long would you indulge?
And sadness a leisure, when would you collude
That want is a master so easy to construe
Where need is a solace we hope will ensue.

A thought so fragile like gossamer, can entangle the mind
Confuses the senses, draws the web, making you blind
The echo of a memory, buried deep within the head
Arouses the thoughts of words that should have been said.

So tomorrow where I will be, lost in my thoughts of what could have been
Picturing scenes of those that made memories, yet the flickering of the eye
Distorts each frame as swiftly they pass by,
As sleep silently creeps in and leaves one only to dream.

The Gentle Fold

Holding hands is a normal natural thing
From babies to toddlers the comforting sling
A reassuring protective safety net
Perhaps through life the best we will ever get.

In haste sometimes we err and go astray
One slip in life and we are made to pay
What price is safety, gone now our shield so true?
Looking back in time at the truth we once knew.

The umbilical cord once cut separates us all
Individuals, but linked as our thread remains true.
Once cusped in hands gently folded around you
Bonding and loving together our cushion should we fall.

Wherever we go we reach out for a hand
Firm fingers, soft palms, yet always sound
The sigh of relief as the comfort is found
The love, trust and faith all in the touch of a hand.

The Little White Lie

How long now since the last lie was told
In distorting the truth is not very bold
To what end does all this deceit lead?
Covering the back all because of greed.

Unlike a spider whose web has to be spun
The first lie sets the path for the lonely one,
To cover the deceit a memory has to be sound
The mind swirls around like the merry go round.

What does it take to remember the truth?
Something that has happened or something uncouth?
Speak as you find is honest, decent and sincere
Your held in respect and admiration this is so clear.

 The lie cheapens you in all that you do
Behind your back others talk about you
It's not very nice and your friends disappear
Being alone and gloomy is what you should fear.

The Mirror

Does the sun rise and make you smile?
Should the mirror reflect all your glory?
Bleary eyed with dark shadows deeply lie
Hair dishevelled tongue dry and all furry.

The mind is nowhere all spinning round like crazy
The eyes from your side everything looks quite hazy,
The mirror is misty wipe it well, it's just the same, oh what the hell!
The span of time to wash and refresh the face

To look into the mirror at the reflection you know so well.
Eyes are dark unfocused and still bleary
The stomach now feels decidedly queasy
Hands do shake and the body feels uneasy

Kneeling by the bowl so deep to say three Hail Marys.
A grumble starts deep within the bowels
Legs do tremble and hands will shake
As the stomach contents make you cough and hake

Not ever again a promise is made to sell the soul.
Shaken and stirred and with weakened resolve
Forgetting now that you have sold your soul,
You look into the mirror now gleaming bright

The image returned stuns you with fright.

The Other Side of Calm

So the knuckles are now swollen, red and raw
The face like a beetroot, flushed and uncomfortably sore
Eyes seem to be on fire as sweat turns to steam
Anger takes over to control and make you look obscene.

What turns the calm into a fierce and stormy sight?
Erodes natural senses changing them into a blight
Rational thinking comes undone and common sense does not prevail
Self- embarrassment on the larger scale wearing the red shroud as the veil.

Heartbeat races, nerves all tight, a pounding headache, a drum like beat
Spittle flying as words tumble from the mouth while stomping hard with the feet
Agitated and with arms akimbo head thrust forward now nose to nose
Punctuating a sentence balance goes tipping forward precariously now on the toes.

To add to the torment of being in the wrong, watched by the encroaching throng
The weight of guilt on shoulders lay overburdened now the balance has all gone.
Staring up from upon the floor being humbled by those eyes that scorn
Rage subsiding and feeling quite depressed wishing that you hadn't been born.

Another time when all is well, a nicer you shows off the other face
Yet to all those who stood and watched the show knows of your disgrace
Each thought that they knew you well; now know that you can never tell
Outside calm waters do not bode well for inside the frame evil torments dwell.

The Silent Weep

Were I to kill a butterfly
I would surely weep
As the loss of a beautiful soul
We can never ever keep.

The beauty has gone forever
A stain upon the floor
When the floor is cleaned
This beauty has gone for evermore.

Should the opera singer reach the scale so high?
The spirit sighs silently in the mind
Can the glory of the music
Reach the angels in the sky?

A memory still lingers
It comes when it is called
Yet the faces, once sharp and so clear
Seem to hang within the shadows

Trying hard to disappear.
Is the doing gone and done now
Is it right to shed a tear?
Now that we carry a heartache

Till the end of time I fear!
Lost in the sea of humanity
Blown across the land
Spinning like the playtoy

Never knowing where to stand.
The voice as clear as crystal
Sharp and precise, you stumble as you turn
Emptiness surrounds you, did you really fall

Or were you looking for they who did call?
The world is full of people
Yet you feel empty and all alone
Walking along crowded avenues not looking at a soul

Eyes rooted to the pavement, aware of what can be said
Labelled quite unfairly, and so you start to wonder,
Is life worth living or is it time that you were dead?
And who would be the first to shed that lonely tear?

True Thoughts are Missing

Where have they all gone, those words I had in my head whilst I was in bed
They summed up my feelings for you that I thought were long ago all dead
They rhymed in the verse emotional and loving that gave me the inner glow
In times of sleep into my mind you do creep, leaving such tenderness I didn't know.

Now I am ensnared I call out your name, my dreams are wanton and you are to blame
In daytime I find my feelings slowly growing and are very hard to contain
Does your body respond to a special moment of which you are so very fond?
Am I asking too much by showing my feelings, if you would in kind respond?

As the time passed since last we met the yearning to be beside you is strong and yet,
How empty the long lonely days understands that passion and pain have to be offset
A comfort is there when I close my eyes to see your face knowing a smile is for me
Whilst a tremble in the stomach asks when close to you I stand are we then meant to
be?

How long then must we be apart before sharing together what's in our hearts?
The changing of feelings is hard to understand where the lifestyle alters to equal parts
The pendulum has shifted now there's two in your mind don't turn away and leave
one behind.
To be truly happy it takes more than two so open your heart and to yourself be kind.

Allow our laughter to echo the streets leave others more joyful whomever we meet
Cast off the shadows that cover us let a lightness come to the soles of the feet
Show off the glow that burns deep inside us let the world see that love is not blind
Follow the dream wherever it leads, if lucky leave the sunbeam for others to find.

True Values

To ask of the question one has to be sure
If the answer is that which you have been waiting for
The negative response could blow an ill wind
Where purpose or triumph you must believe in.

An ambition is good yet really two fold
To sacrifice all others or so I am told
A single path that has to be trod
Devoid of all friendship is a lonely plod.

Now greed is the factor for money alone
A single entity with numbers you wish to clone,
A healthy bank balance is a very nice thing
But without friendship life has no zing.

In sickness and in health not forgoing the stealth
Should a marriage take place is it for love or the wealth?
Fear strikes within knowing perhaps that you have to share
Leaves one all ailing and poorly now full of despair.

Twilight

In the twilight of my years
More fonder of love I shed tears
My memories under oak trees spread
Of the future that I fearful dread.

An empty soul, eyes dried from tears bled
A sob in the throat unable to shed
A beat with no rhythm pounds within the breast
The heart does a flutter deep in the chest

Yet lonesome in life is not there by chance.
A choice before thee one decision to make
Along which pathway which one to take
One of the silver the other of brass

Which is the greener, which is the crass?
A swirling grey cloud full laden with rain
Under the oak tree, a shelter to gain
Yet in autumn, no leaves offer kindness

No shelter from the cold stinging pain.
The shiver, a tremble, a gust of cold wind
No sound from the birds, no call or a cry
The shoulders slump forward from the weight of the rain

From the throat a sound comes, a moan and a sigh.
Thunder rolls and forked lightening crackles
Under the oak tree a sodden form cackles
Delirious, tormented or just plain mad

The decision was made on the path that was tread

Umbilical Memory

Did a ripple of laughter make me smile?
While inside a warm sensation stirred
A happy feeling crept up upon me
So joyful and content I was immersed.

A tiny warm hand entered mine
Little fingers tightly clasped
A gentle tugging, insistence sublime
To join their play was gloriously divine.

Sandcastles on the beach, so proud you both were
Lilos in the pool, all day with water wings
Shivering at the end of the day, warm towels felt like fur
All night talking about the day's fun and other things.

The sun slowly sinks as night descends
Stories read and eyelids droop,
A memory is made but will it be remembered?
As time emptily passes who is to say that it has all been ended?

Unashamed Desire

So it seems that you are within me, in my head and in my dreams
My emotions are changing more frequently, or so it seems
There's dryness in my mouth and my mind calls out your name
Night times I share tender moments with you for this I carry no shame.

Should I dare speak to you I wonder what you will say
Tomorrow will never come though I long for this each day
How shallow then should I be if I were to turn away from you
When this could be the right thing the one that could be true.

Walk with me and tell me the words that I long to hear
Explain to me your feelings if they are there for me my dear?
I hurt inside when missing you I long to hold your hand
I need to tell you everything so you will understand.

The silence is quite deafening I want to hear your sweet hello
The cheery morning greeting as all in a hurry swiftly do you go
Leaving me this shapely vision, the curvy contours which really do entice
A sense of anticipation as the apple offered tentatively, a flavour full of spice.

I want to hold you in my arms to feel your comforting embrace
Inhale the fragrance of your hair, taste the sweetness of your lips
As emotions build up inside of me, to be as one with you I wish to haste
No longer do I want a mirage, I want you as my woman, to hold and to kiss.

Undying Love

Now my youth has gone and left me
And I'm standing here on my own
Four walls that surround me
Is the place now that I call home.

Yet no memories are abiding
No warmth is there to share
For my loved ones are behind me
I know not if they care.

Yet my love for them is no burden
It will be there till the day I die
As we look up to the heavens
We forget how big the sky.

So no man shall stop my dreaming
That has all been in the past
Of all the childish, memories
That grew to last and last.

So forgive me if I fail to smile at you
For my mind is in the past
Should happiness again remind me?
Once more to enjoy fully the past.

Perhaps one day you will see me
With a far away look in my eye
I'm thinking of my loved ones I so long to see
And trying so very hard to hold back a sigh.

All of us must enjoy love each step along the way
Never forgetting we have a future, living only for today
We must cherish every moment along life's highway
Remember someone's already been there and paved for us the way.

Unknown

Do you see me as a single star shaped snowflake
That melts when touching the warmth of the skin
Or fashioned from the burning embers which fades and turns grey as sin
Perhaps as a solitary raindrop that forms the regal crown just before it breaks.

Do you see me as the nimbus cloud suspended in the bright blue sky?
The twinkling star that catches your eye in the dead of night
Or the beam of the laser made by man that gives you the fright?
The silent blackness of the night briefly lit up by the comet streaking by?

Blown by the gentle breeze where the destination is unknown
Swirling and turning through dales and across rivers, over hills and through the vales
Could it be the prism holding firmly in its grip the colours of the rainbow so they are
    not alone?
Silently it travels collecting wisdom on its way storing this forever as this is not for
    sale.

In the world of mortals where solid objects mean more than most
In using all their senses to survive image how they would react should they see a
    ghost?
So should the ray of sunlight bring warmth to their cooling skin?
Would they be happy to feel it as this is what they want to call as their only sin?

Visions with You

Is life all tired and lonely, why no, for there is always you
A sigh of the wind as through the trees it blew
A swoosh of the sea as it breaks upon the sand
Or the rustle of leaves as on the ground they land.

The ray of sunlight brings warmth to the skin
Eyes beam with delight as a memory begins
The sound of a raindrop splashing on a window pane
A wondrous feeling that can be replayed again and again.

To capture a thought one has to have hope
The emotional mystery vision, intrigue also the scope
An ache in the heart a feeling that cannot be taught
Imagine a picture of the future, calm peaceful never distraught.

One has to be there for a memory too share
To enjoy all the feelings to have someone who will care
In moments such as this being able to share and enjoy bliss
A peal of kind laughter before sealing love with a kiss.

What's in a Face?

A smile brings glowing warmth to the soul
The twinkle in the eyes you have the goal
That tingles on the lips waiting for the kiss
Pulse now racing, will you ever get your wish.

Sweet as the taste of wine, fresh inviting and divine
Warmth of the cheek subtle tenderness of the smile
Eyes shining with love, now forever you are mine
Lips wet and a glossy cherry red waiting for a while.

The furrowed brow and eyebrows arched
A distasteful look of sour disparagement
Lips turned down all sullen you're guilty as charged
Behind the eyes though a slight glint of encouragement.

The face is a transcript which has to be read
Words are not needed it is the interpretation instead
So sweet and angelic or the devil incarnate
The attraction or detraction between love and the hate.

Where are you Dad?

Where have you gone Dad why did you leave us at home?
Alone with my sister and a not so nice Mum
I saw you this morning as I went out to roam
Upon my return you had gone I was left all alone.

What have we done Dad to be left in despair?
Each evening we look for you, we see your empty chair
If we have hurt you we are sorry-okay?
We need you back beside us for all of our days.

Who can we talk too for a secret to keep?
Who can we now look up to with Angelic faces so sweet?
Dad this is torment tell us what did we do?
If we said we didn't love you then this is untrue.

We do have a memory but that's not enough
We both need you here to hold us and to give us your love
We only have one Dad and I'm afraid it is you
Come home please Dad make our dreams come true.

White Feathers

The parable says turn the other cheek but inside the pain is buried too deep
Time heals the pain, yet who nurses the ache or the ill fate that we rake?
It is inside the head where the spectres are sent remorseless and forever to keep
The tricks of the mind nobody sees whilst seeking sanity is too much to take.

Chafed sore cheeks, red from slaps eyes a misty haze yet physically you can't engage
Frustration is overbearing the pride has all gone something occurs to bring on the rage
Something inside snaps and your world does collapse turning aside you want to hide
Not understanding courage yet feeling fear suffering torment and torture deep inside.

With sallow complexion and white shaking hands nobody cares or understands
The horrors and destruction the waste of human life yet war is all over save the blood
    in the sand
Walking past dusty dishevelled people through deserted towns leaving war behind
Ears still ringing from bullets whistling by dark secrets forever the eyes now hide.

Long years have passed yet the dreams continue, still they haunt
Peace is with the believer so each Sunday sanctuary in church is sought,
On this day an envelope is opened a memento from the war it is thought
A tear flows from the misty eye, and upon the white feathers it will be caught.

It is not for celebration or a bravery reward quite the opposite it is known
To signify the act of cowardice this was sent straight to the soldiers' home
An unknown desk clerk sent it on orders from high above
So the envelope is put upon the fire to save the shame from those he does love.

Who am I?

Perhaps it is unfair to mock, scoff or to scorn
About the size of the head with which we were born
For inside the shell, all covered in gel is there that I am
To function and work for the body the best way that I can.

Without me you see, you are just flesh and bone
You cannot survive here all on your own
Whatever you do or don't do is all down to me
Each movement you make I can guarantee.

I make you think, speak and even let you see
To calculate movement exactly and quite regularly
Each thought for your life has to be planned
To the tiniest of details for the movement of a hand.

Some heads can be as oval or round as a drum
Others, unfortunately, small, the size of a pea
Yet one common factor that prejudice must overcome
Is the brain and its function in life that we cannot see.

So if you have a bald scalp, or a full head of hair
The quirks of fate is that both of you share
A vital necessity all of which is exactly the same
Names simply vary but the real one is that of the Brain.

Willow

I see you standing strong, supple, tall yet silvery too
Your roots are unseen yet travel deep down and true
Enjoying each single raindrop as the giver of life
Forever the sentinel withstanding all trouble and strife.

Alone all seasons you stand as a beacon for our land
With regal majesty you overlook the country side, vale and dale
Sighing gently as the winds in gusts or storms prevail
From twig to trunk as flexible as a cloud forever you must stand.

Sweeping over brooks and rivers you are a wonderful sight
Ideal for picnic spots and a hot summer's grateful shade
A children's favourite climbing frame a place for delight
You see babies grow to adults, these mortal visions you cannot trade.

Inside you have the sap, life giver for longevity humans would love to tap
Should they stand still for eternity would the willows understand that?
How envy wracks the human mind to live forever, and so they cut you down
Smug in their done deeds they leave you, forgetting the roots deep within the ground.

Wistful Memory

Ah! Youth, how I remember you so well old friend
Slick and trim, smart well dressed and good looking
Was it actually me that followed each fashion trend?
Talent at spotting bargains and elusive to police bookings.

Sweet rendezvous' encounters pleasurably spent in time honoured ways
Oh how we miss those long lazy, languid, sunny, warm days
Trouble free evenings down at the pub, a few pints then away for grub
Laughing and joking on the way home pretending your sober you trip over a tub.

Money in the pocket and good thoughts inside the head
Staying at the girlfriends sure that that is what she said
Going to the movies in the back row, on this there were no regrets
Delicious times and fond memories, did you see her after that or simply forget?

Broken hearts aplenty, some of these also applied to you
Each time you found a new love, for sure that this one, was true
How life makes you miss each turn and curve, along the straight road one must travel
As we go through life only then will the real true story begin to unravel.

Each milestone of age is a page within the book yet sometimes forgotten, overlooked
A wife and children too, seeing you through their eyes remembering liberties that you
    took
Now they have grown and settled into their youth your back into the memory again
Smiling more to yourself as you recall both the pangs of pleasure and the hurt of pain.

Worthy

In the silence of the night when all is still
My thoughts become focused upon you and what could be
The ache deep inside fails to go away
So forever while apart the pain will stay.

How hard must I strive to be worthy of you?
The shortfalls in abundance keep me all askew
What can I offer in terms of years of love?
Financially unstable insufficient enough.

Where once in confidence through life I strode
With head held high on par with whom I spoke
The lifetime of knowledge seems all have departed
Self esteem so low life now is all in darkness.

To offer my hand, my life, my soul
With limited ambition, knowledge of no other goals
To tender a love is not worthy for you
Remains in deep silence hidden away from view.

In watching your passing the pain in my eye
I turn away quickly so you never see that I cry
For now that I know I will never be free
As you are the chosen one, forever for me.

If clever I could be with endearing words which would set me free
No odes or laments would ever cease
As the light clears away shadows the brightness allows me to see
The mind and the soul will be injected with life, again to be in peace.

You

Yes, it is you that I think of every day
It is you who is in my mind each moment
Yours is the face I see in the crowd
Yet, when I try to touch you, always
you are out of reach.

Time has passed and you have grown
Memories have dimmed and I am now
The father you wish that you'd rather
Would not have known.

Of you I still hold dear, the days of
Your childhood as I watched you grow.
The smile on your face, the twinkle in your eye
That showed you loved me so.

Birthdays and Christmas's come and go
Love and laughter always showed
There is always inside, a warm glow
My pride in you I showed for all to know.

Tears and heartache you have suffered
Alone you think you are,
Adrift in the mad sad world,
In your younger days whom did you turn too?

When you were frightened, you shed a tear
I dried it and brought you cheer
A smile made things better
As you drove away all your fear.

At night I stood at your bedside as you slept
You had no fears or nightmares then
The sleep was peaceful and contented
A smile on your lips of a happy memory.

You needed me then as I needed you
Times may have changed, yet,
The need is still there along with the love
My love for you has not diminished by the passage of time

Yes it is you that I think of each moment of the day.